Knights and Castles

Written by Jason Hook
Illustrated by Adam Hook

MARKS &
SPENCER

Marks and Spencer p.l.c.
Baker Street, London W1U 8EP
www.marksandspencer.com

Copyright © Exclusive Editions 2001

This book was created by Monkey Puzzle Media Ltd

ISBN 1-84273-194-7

Printed in Dubai

Designer: Sarah Crouch
Cover design: Victoria Webb
Editor: Jon Richards
Artwork commissioning:
Roger Goddard-Coote
Project manager: Alex Edmonds

Contents

What was a motte-and-bailey?

MANY OF THE FIRST NORMAN CASTLES HAD A WOODEN BUILDING, called a keep, built on a high mound called a 'motte'. This was protected by a ditch and a wall of earth, which also surrounded a courtyard known as the 'bailey'. This was called a motte-and-bailey castle.

Who carried a portable castle?

When the Normans, led by William the Conqueror, invaded England in 1066, they brought with them the wooden parts of a portable castle. They landed at Pevensey, in East Sussex, and had put their castle together by the following day.

What did you do if the king wanted to build a castle on your land?

You moved! When William the Conqueror had Lincoln Castle built in 1068, a total of 166 houses were pulled down to make room for it.

How did William conquer England?

By building strong castles, William was able to conquer a nation of 1,000 000 people with a force of only 7,000 men. The English at this time had few castles from which they could defend their land.

Which tapestry shows a castle?

The Bayeux Tapestry, started in 1067, shows William's men building a castle at Hastings. Two of the builders appear to be settling an argument – by fighting with their shovels!

DEVILS AND WICKED MEN

A writer living at the time of the Normans noted: 'They filled the whole land with these castles. They sorely burdened the unhappy people of the country with forced labour on the castles. And when the castles were made, they filled them with devils and wicked men'.

Which bishop designed the Tower of London?

A Norman Knight

T HE WHITE TOWER, THE OLDEST PART OF
THE TOWER OF LONDON, WAS BUILT
for William in 1078. It was designed by Gandulf, the Bishop
of Rochester. He had earned a reputation for designing
castles by building one beside his cathedral.

What did you do if the king visited your castle?

You welcomed him warmly!
William had made it law that he
could occupy the castle of any of
his barons whenever he wished.

A LOOK AT THE BOOK

William wished to know exactly what he had conquered. So in 1087
his surveyors produced the Domesday Book, which recorded the
sources of rent and taxes in his kingdom. It listed estates, livestock and
49 different castles.

How important were castles?

A writer of the twelfth century
described Britain's royal castles as
the 'bones of the kingdom'.

How many men did it take to build a castle?

IN 1296 CAERNARVON CASTLE WAS UNDER CONSTRUCTION BY EUROPE'S FINEST castle architect, Master James of St George. His workers included 400 stonemasons, 1,000 labourers, 200 carters and 30 carpenters and metalworkers. In the summer of the previous year there were also some 3,500 builders working on Beaumaris Castle.

Which king's builders went on strike?

In 1303 carpenters and ditchers refused to work for King Edward I at Dunfermline Castle because he owed them so much money for work on his other castles.

How long did it take to build a castle?

Wooden motte-and bailey castles could be built in under a fortnight, but stone castles were a different matter. One of Edward's Welsh castles, Harlech, took over seven years to complete and builders worked on Beaumaris Castle for 35 years without finishing it.

What machines did builders use?

The only machines medieval builders had to help them construct their amazing castles were simple cranes, pulleys and wheelbarrows.

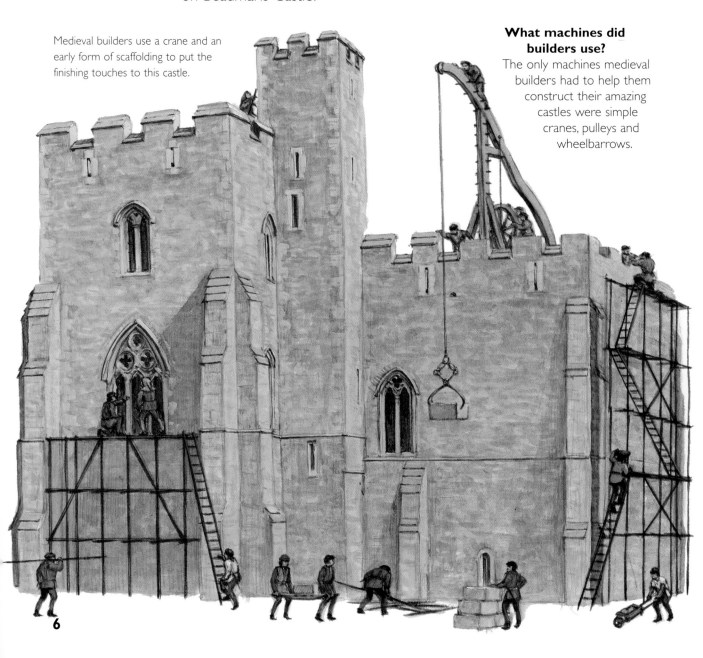

Medieval builders use a crane and an early form of scaffolding to put the finishing touches to this castle.

Were castle walls always grey?

L IME WAS SOMETIMES USED TO PAINT
castle walls white so that their dazzling towers could be seen from miles away. This was how the White Tower at the Tower of London got its name. Henry III ordered longer gutters for the Tower, to stop rainwater marking its white walls.

A medieval stone castle

Why did castle staircases spiral clockwise?
A clockwise spiral staircase allowed a defender to retreat backwards up the stairs while swinging his sword with his right hand at a pursuer below. It was almost impossible for the man chasing him to swing a blow – unless he was left-handed!

How thick were castle walls?
Stone castles were built with walls over three metres thick. These could withstand missiles fired from enormous catapults. At Dover Castle, in Kent, some walls were over six metres thick.

What did gargoyles spit out at Beaumaris Castle?
At Beaumaris, sewage from the garderobes travelled down shafts then out through the mouths of carved gargoyles and into the moat. In 1306 there were complaints that the gargoyles' mouths had become blocked.

Why did the castle moat stink?
The 'garderobes', or castle toilets, were small, stone rooms with a hole in the floor. They were often positioned over a shaft that led directly into the moat.

DRESS TO IMPRESS

Kings could force labourers to work on their castles. During Edward III's building work at Windsor Castle, stonemasons had to travel down from Yorkshire. They were made to dress in bright red clothes – so that they could not sneak away.

Bees buzzing around their bee-hive.

BUTTER BY DESIGN

In medieval times English kings also ruled lands in France. Richard the Lionheart built a magnificent castle called Château Gaillard in Normandy. He was so pleased with its design that he boasted he could defend the castle even if its walls were made of butter.

Were castles fit for kings and queens?

At Windsor Castle, Edward III had six private chambers, one large enough to contain 20 windows and another painted in azure, gold, green and vermillion. The queen had four chambers, including a dancing room and a chamber covered with mirrors.

Where were bees kept?

Bees were kept in straw hives on the castle walls. Their honey was used to sweeten food and drink.

How did they tell the time at Windsor Castle?

Windsor Castle contained the first mechanical clock known in England.

Which king had double-glazing?

As the medieval period went on, more and more castles installed glass in their windows. Henry III even had double-glazing at Windsor Castle.

How did people grow grapes?

In the 1100s Gerald of Wales describes his estate at Manorbier Castle as including a deep fish-pond, a beautiful orchard and a vineyard. The climate in medieval times was slightly hotter than today, and conditions were ideal for growing grapes to make wine.

Who lived in castles?

CASTLES WERE NORMALLY THE HOMES OF KINGS AND barons, rather than knights. But royalty only visited a castle occasionally, before moving on to the next of their many homes. During their visits the castle became home to crowds of workers, cooks and servants.

A royal party arrives at a castle, announced by a herald.

Were pets kept in castles?
Yes, lords and ladies kept pets including dogs, cats, squirrels, mice, songbirds and even monkeys, bears and leopards. They also had horses, hounds and hawks for hunting, which was the favourite pastime of most lords.

Where did a king keep his elephant?

A S WELL AS BEING A CASTLE FORTRESS, THE TOWER OF LONDON WAS AN important prison and a zoo for exotic animals! In one of the towers, called the Lion Tower, Henry III kept an elephant.

A medieval king watches while his queen feeds her pet monkey.

How did a king communicate with his servants?
Henry III had a speaking tube known as the 'king's ear' through which he could talk to his servants. It linked the king's solar, or private chamber, with the great hall at Winchester Castle.

What services did serfs perform for the castle?

Serfs living around the castle were given different duties to help with building, maintaining and defending the castle. At one castle a villager had to fetch basins of water so that the knights could wash. In return, he received bread, wine and the first choice of kitchen scraps.

How were taxes paid?

The peasants who lived on the lord's land had to visit the castle to pay their taxes. These included the 'wood-penny' tax which people paid for the right to collect firewood from the estate's forests.

Who lived around the castle?

MANY PEASANTS LIVED AROUND THE CASTLE WALLS, BECAUSE IT WAS A place of security in dangerous times. The castle estate also provided land for farmers. Many of them were 'serfs', who were owned and controlled by the lord on whose land they worked. The serfs farmed the lord's land and raised livestock. They divided their produce between the lord and themselves.

Who travelled with trunks?

Serfs living on the estate of Bamburgh Castle, Northumberland, were expected to bring a tree trunk to the castle once a year to help with building works. This tax was known as 'trunkage'.

Serfs work in the fields around the castle.

GOING, GOING, GONG

In a medieval castle the toilet was known as the 'gong'. The 'gong farmer' was the servant who emptied the pits at the bottom of the latrines, using a bucket and shovel. In 1326 a gong farmer named Richard the Raker died after falling into one of these pits!

Did castle servants live in squalor?

Not necessarily. At Sir John Fastolf's castle at Caister, in Norfolk, the cook, gardener and porter each had separate bedrooms – equipped with feather beds, sheets and curtains.

Who needed plenty of trousers?

A SERVANT CALLED THE ALE CONNER TESTED THE castle's beer by pouring it onto a wooden bench then sitting in it. If he soon found himself glued to the bench, he declared that the ale was bad. If he could stand up, he declared the ale to be good.

A castle mill

How did a windmill turn a profit?

Many castles, such as Edward I's castle at Dover, had their own windmills. Peasants had to grind their corn at the lord's windmill, and, in return, the lord kept some of the flour. They also had to pay to bake bread in the castle oven!

Who was allowed to fish?

The lord of the manor only allowed certain people to fish in the ponds on the castle estate. One lord only gave fishing rights to pregnant women!

How did Edward I keep himself amused?

Edward I travelled to his daughter's wedding in 1296 with entertainers including his personal jester called Tom the Fool, a fiddler, a female acrobat, three actors and a bagpipe player.

The king's jester

How big were the ovens in the castle kitchen?

King John ordered new kitchens to be built at his castles, with ovens big enough to roast two or three oxen.

Which groom died from indigestion?

At the wedding feast of Prince Lionel in 1368, 30 courses were served. The food included suckling pig with crab, heron with carp, eel pies, peacocks with cabbage, pickled ox-tongue and meats covered with gold leaf. The bloated groom died four months later.

Who looked after the jesters?

After 1502, there was an official in the royal household called the Keeper of the King's Fools.

Did jesters wear shoes with curly toes?

A jester at the court of William Rufus was known as 'Horner' because he stuffed the long toes of his shoes and curled them up like a ram's horn.

Were kings really entertained by jesters?

YES, MANY KINGS KEPT DWARVES, FOOLS AND JESTERS TO MAKE THEM LAUGH at feasts and celebrations. One jester was granted an estate in Suffolk on condition that he entertained Henry II each Christmas with 'a leap, a whistle and a fart'.

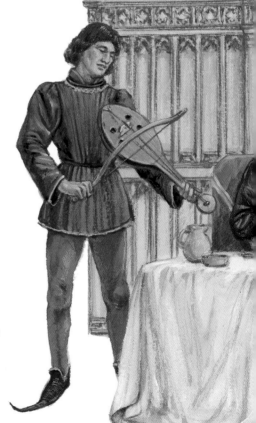

Why were there sharks' teeth on salt-cellars?

Kings and lords lived in fear of being poisoned, and employed tasters to test their food. Sharks' teeth, known as 'serpents' tongues', were believed to sweat when placed near poisonous food.

Did people have table manners?

One book advised diners: 'It is improper to scratch your head on the table; to remove from your neck fleas and other vermin and kill them in front of others; and to scratch or pull at scabs.' Another advised against stroking cats and dogs beneath the table.

Were there really 'four and twenty blackbirds baked in a pie'?

Yes there were. As a novelty, castle chefs sometimes baked an empty pie then lifted off the crust and filled it with live birds before serving. Roast swans and peacocks were also put back into their skins for presentation.

WINE INTO WATER

A deep well was vital in a castle to supply drinking water during a siege. When Exeter Castle was besieged in 1136 and their water ran out, the occupants of the castle used wine to drink, bake bread and put out fires.

Were castle meals fit for a king?

THEY CERTAINLY COULD BE! PREPARING TO SPEND THE CHRISTMAS OF 1206 at Winchester Castle, King John ordered the local sheriff to provide 1,500 chickens, 5,000 eggs, 20 oxen, 100 pigs and 100 sheep. Henry III made more exotic demands for a banquet at Gloucester, which included 10,000 eels, 36 swans, 34 peacocks and 90 boars.

Lord, ladies, bishops and barons enjoy a feast fit for a king.

Which bishop escaped from the Tower of London?

THE BISHOP OF DURHAM, RANULF FLAMBARD, BECAME THE FIRST prisoner to escape from the Tower of London, where he was imprisoned in 1106. He sent out for some food and drink, then offered wine to his gaolers until they fell asleep. Ranulf then used a rope, which had been concealed in a wine barrel, to lower himself through a window to the ground. His servants were waiting with a boat on the Thames, and the bishop escaped to France.

What instruments of torture were used in castle dungeons?

Racks stretched victims until their limbs popped from their sockets; thumbscrews and iron boots crushed thumbs and feet; hot irons branded the flesh; pincers tore nails from fingers; bridles held a prisoner's tongue; and a press crushed a prisoner's whole body, with more weights added each day until he or she confessed.

What was an oubliette?

Oubliette comes from the French word meaning 'forgotten'. The oubliette was a tiny cell at the back of the castle dungeon where unwanted prisoners were thrown and forgotten.

How were rich prisoners treated?

They were often treated as guests and kept in great comfort in the castle until a ransom was paid for them. Some prisoners even signed an agreement, promising to behave chivalrously at the castle until their ransom was received.

How did people stand trial?

In the early Middle Ages, some people accused of a crime faced 'trial by ordeal'. They had to grip a bar of red-hot iron. Their burns were then bandaged for three days. When they were unwrapped, any sign of infection proved that they were guilty.

Why should a serf return a hawk?

Hawking was a favourite pastime of the rich. Any serf who found a hawk and failed to return it to its wealthy owner was punished by having the bird peck six ounces of flesh from his breast.

A prisoner in his dungeon hugs himself to try and keep warm.

How was someone hung, drawn and quartered?

Traitors were first 'hung', then cut down before they died. Next they were 'drawn', having their intestines cut out and held up in front of them. When they finally died, their bodies were 'quartered' – cut into four pieces.

A thief sits in the stocks, covered with the rotting fruit and vegetables that passers-by have thrown at him.

Who had their ears nailed?

Thieves were locked into wooden frames, called stocks or

pillories, where people could pelt them with rotten fruit. Sometimes, their ears were nailed to the wood.

Whose screams were heard from Berkeley Castle?

On the night of September 21, 1327, the disgraced King Edward II was murdered in the dungeon at Berkeley Castle in Gloucestershire. His screams could be heard from the village beyond the castle walls.

THE YOUNG PRINCES

The skeletons of two young boys were found buried in the Tower of London in 1674. They were thought to be the sons of Edward IV, 12-year-old Edward and 10-year-old Richard. The young princes had disappeared in 1483, enabling Richard III to take the throne.

What was 'Greek Fire'?

WHEN ATTACKING A CASTLE, SOME ARMIES USED AN explosive material known as 'Greek Fire'. It was placed in jars and barrels and fired from catapults to explode among the castle inhabitants. Greek Fire contained sulphur, tartar, pitch, salt and oil. One observer noted that it smelt foul and could only be put out with vinegar. It was also sometimes fired from hand pumps – the first flamethrowers!

This enormous catapult could hurl huge boulders over or into castle walls.

Did you need much equipment to besiege a castle?
A book published in England in 1489 said that you needed the following equipment to lay siege to a castle: 248 guns; 13,500 kg of gunpowder; 2,200 stones; 200,000 crossbow quarrels; 1,000 shovels and 200 lanterns.

Who set light to cats, mice and birds?
One medieval expert on sieges suggested tying burning ropes to cats and mice, and sending these 'incendiary animals' into a besieged castle through the drains. In the 1260s Simon de Montfort planned to set light to London by tying flaming torches to the talons of birds.

Who ordered some pigs?
When besieging Rochester Castle in 1215, King John sent an order for 'forty bacon pigs of the fattest and least good for eating, to bring fire beneath the tower'.

How were messages returned?
At the siege of Auberoche in 1345, a messenger was caught sneaking messages out from the besieged castle. His messages were hung around his neck, and he was placed in the sling of a catapult and fired back over the castle walls.

What use is a dead horse?
In 1339 French attackers besieging Edward III's castle at Flanders launched dead horses and cattle over the walls. A painting from this time shows a horse being fired from a catapult.

When did it rain manure?
At a siege in 1422 the attackers used a catapult to fire 2,000 cartloads of manure over the castle walls.

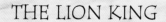

THE LION KING

At the siege of Roxburgh in 1460, James II of Scotland was killed by a Lion! One of his own bombards – which was known as The Lion – exploded, and a piece of the barrel cut his thigh-bone in two.

How did a mine work?
Miners from an attacking army dug a mine, or tunnel, beneath the walls of a besieged castle, propping up the walls of the mine with wooden supports. The miners then filled the tunnel with brushwood and grease and set light to it. The props burnt, the tunnel collapsed and the castle wall above it fell into the hole.

Soldiers set light to the fuse of a bombard.

What is Muckle Meg?

BOMBARDS WERE ENORMOUS cannons used to fire missiles at castle walls, making a noise that could be heard over 6.5 km away. One famous example can still be seen at Edinburgh Castle. It weighs 6,000 kg and is called Mons Meg, or 'the great iron murderer Muckle Meg'.

DON'T BE SQUARE

Early castles had square towers, which were easily damaged by catapults and had a narrow range of vision. Later castles were built with round towers. These deflected missiles and gave the defenders a much better view of their attackers.

How did straw kill a knight in armour?

In 1417 Sir Edward Springhouse tried to scale the walls of the castle at Caen, in France, but the defenders pushed his ladder away. He fell to the ground and lay as helpless in his heavy armour as an upturned tortoise. So the French dropped burning straw on him and roasted him alive!

How useful were moats?

The castle moat was an excellent defence, as it had to be filled in before attackers could reach the castle walls. The moat also prevented miners tunnelling beneath the castle walls, because it flooded their tunnels.

A moated castle with specially designed round towers.

A soldier pours boiling water through a murder-hole on to an enemy.

Who tried to barge into a castle?

Kenilworth Castle was so well defended by the waters of a lake and moat that when Henry III's son Prince Edward attacked it in 1266, he had to use barges to reach the walls.

What was a murder-hole?

A MURDER-HOLE WAS A GAP IN THE CEILING OF A PASSAGEWAY, particularly in the castle gate-house. The defenders in rooms above the passage could drop missiles down through the murder-hole on to attackers who had entered below.

Castle inhabitants attempt to foil the battering-ram by softening its blow with an enormous 'cushion'.

Did castle defenders use siege engines?

Yes, at the siege of Kenilworth Castle both attackers and defenders fired so many rocks that many of them collided and shattered in mid-air.

Why did the garrison put down dishes of water?

If attackers tried to tunnel under the castle walls, then the vibrations they caused would create ripples in the dishes of water, alerting the soldiers in the besieged castle.

How do you stop a battering-ram battering?

SOMETIMES THE CASTLE INHABITANTS lowered down enormous 'cushions' filled with feathers, rope and wool, to soften the blows of the battering-ram. They also used an enormous forked stick to stop the ram from swinging.

Who used chemical warfare?

Some castle defenders used chemical warfare by throwing gas bombs made from sulphur, pitch and horses' hooves! These landed among attackers and released their choking fumes.

Why were dove-cotes built into castle walls?

Doves were used to send messages, which was often the only way to send for help when a castle was surrounded and under siege.

19

How did squires get big muscles?

They practised fighting using weapons which had extra weights added, so that the exercise made them stronger.

What were pages and squires?

WHEN THEY WERE SEVEN YEARS OLD, THE SONS OF

knights and nobles were often sent to the household of a lord to serve as a 'page'. The page waited at table, and learned how to behave properly at the castle. At the age of 14, the page might become a 'squire', the personal servant of a knight. He assisted him at war and in tournaments, and learned how to fight, joust, hunt, sing and dance – so that one day he too could become a knight.

What was a quintain?

The quintain was a revolving dummy with a shield on one side and a sword or sandbag on the other. A squire practised jousting by striking the dummy's shield, but had to ride past quickly enough or the sandbag would swing around and knock him off his horse.

How were pages expected to behave?

One book advised pages: 'Do not sigh, or belch, or with puffing and blowing cast foul breath upon your lord.'

Did pages do any cleaning?

Yes, they did many household chores. But they were advised: 'Do not lick a dish with your tongue to get at the dust.'

Squires fight one another piggyback, to build strength and weaponry skills.

At the end of a long apprenticeship, this squire is knighted.

What was a knight?

A KNIGHT WAS AN ARMOURED WARRIOR WHO FOUGHT ON horseback. Knights swore an oath of loyalty to a lord. They promised to fight for him, and, in exchange, they received land, money and protection from the lord.

How was a squire knighted?

Having completed his apprenticeship, a squire bathed, dressed in a white robe, and spent a night alone in solemn vigil, or prayer. He was then presented with his spurs, shield and sword by an older knight, who gently touched the squire's cheek or neck with his sword.

Why would a squire avoid being knighted?

Becoming a knight was a very expensive business. Some squires preferred to remain as they were, because it was much cheaper.

Why did the Earl of Suffolk knight a French squire?

The Earl was captured by the squire during a battle. Embarrassed to be the prisoner of a mere squire, he knighted the Frenchman.

WINNING HIS SPURS

Receiving his spurs was a sign that a squire had become a knight. Edward III's son, Edward Prince of Wales, became known as the Black Prince when he wore a black surcoat and carried a black shield at the Battle of Crécy in 1357. When asked to help his son in battle, Edward III replied: 'Let the boy win his spurs'.

21

What was an 'arming doublet'?

A knight wore a leather jacket called an arming doublet, which was covered with laces. These were used to tie on the knight's many pieces of armour.

Could a knight move in his armour?

YES, ALTHOUGH HIS ARMOUR OFTEN WEIGHED OVER 20 KG THE weight was evenly spread. Medieval manuscripts describe fully armoured knights turning cartwheels and leaping into the saddle.

How good was a castle's armoury?

An armoury inventory was compiled in 1343, when the Earl of Huntingdon handed over Dover Castle to Sir Bartholomew Burghersh. It lists 50 bows (two generations old); 22 ancient helmets (covered with rotten leather); 25 coats of mail (rusty); 25 antique gauntlets (decayed); 103 shields (34 unserviceable); 6 buckets of arrows (without feathers); 118 lances (18 without heads).

Was it hot in a suit of armour?

It was so hot and difficult to breathe that knights actually died from suffocation in the heat and dust of battle. At the Battle of Agincourt in 1415, many knights, including the Duke of York, suffocated in the mud beneath a huge pile of French bodies.

A knight demonstrates just how agile it is possible to be wearing armour.

How was a knight's horse kept peaceful?

A knight's horse wore as much armour as the knight. Some knights also gave their horses wax ear-plugs so that they were not scared by the noise of battle.

Why did priests fight with maces?

The Church prohibited priests from drawing blood with a sword. So many of them used blunt maces instead.

Who rode blindly into battle?

The King of Bohemia rode into the Battle of Crécy against the English, but his horse had to be guided by his knights because the king was completely blind.

SPACE SUIT

When NASA was designing lightweight, flexible spacesuits for their astronauts, they studied the suit of armour worn in combat by Henry VIII.

How powerful was a longbow?

ONE WELSH ARCHER FIRED AN ARROW FROM A LONGBOW WHICH PASSED through a knight's chainmail leggings, his thigh and his saddle, and finally killed his horse.

An archer prepares to let an arrow fly from his longbow.

Why do people stick up two fingers?

This insulting gesture originated with a French threat to chop off the two fingers used by English archers to draw their longbows. When the archers helped to win a great English victory at Agincourt in 1415, they taunted the French by sticking up their two fingers to show that they still had them!

Who wore exploding armour?

At some tournaments knights wore spring-loaded panels of armour during a joust. The armour exploded into fragments if it was successfully struck by the lance of an opponent.

Why did knights wear tokens?

IT WAS CONSIDERED CHIVALROUS FOR A KNIGHT TO PERFORM BRAVE DEEDS

out of a spiritual or 'courtly' love for a lady. Many knights wore tokens of their lady, such as a sleeve or garter, to show their loyalty.

A knight accepts a token of love from his lady.

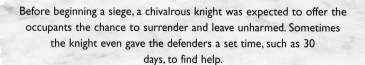

KNIGHT TIME

Before beginning a siege, a chivalrous knight was expected to offer the occupants the chance to surrender and leave unharmed. Sometimes the knight even gave the defenders a set time, such as 30 days, to find help.

What was chivalry?

Chivalry was a set of rules which outlined the way in which a knight was supposed to behave. According to the laws of chivalry a knight was expected to be loyal to his lord, to defend the Church, to use his sword to defend widows, orphans and the poor and to be gentle and courteous.

Which king wore a garter?

When the Countess of Salisbury dropped her blue garter, Edward III picked it up and put it on. To celebrate the occasion he formed a society at Windsor Castle for his most chivalrous knights, called the Order of the Garter.

Where did the three lions come from?

The three lions, which are the coat-of-arms of England as well as the badge of the national football team, were first used on the shield of Richard the Lionheart.

Why did a knight wear a turnip?

Canting was a type of heraldry where a knight's coat-of-arms was based on his name. One knight called Rand, which means turnip, proudly decorated his shield with a picture of a turnip

This knight has his coat-of-arms on his shield and lance banner, as well as on the horse's coat.

Who wore a flower-pot on his head?

Knights wore crests on their helmets to show their coat-of-arms. Crests were very elaborate. One Knight of the Garter wore a crest designed to look like a flower-pot with a plant growing from it.

What was the job of a herald?

Heralds kept records of the different coats-of-arms and recorded the deeds of knights during a battle. They also conducted tournaments and kept score in the contests between the knights.

How did a tree of chivalry work?

At tournaments different coloured shields were hung from a 'tree of chivalry'. By touching a shield of a certain colour, the knight's herald selected whichever type of combat his lord wished to fight.

How did heraldry work?

KNIGHTS ALL LOOKED THE SAME COVERED IN ARMOUR. SO A system of heraldry was developed by which knights could be recognized. It used designs called coats-of-arms which they wore on their shields, their coats, and the coats of their horses.

When were 2,500 knights held for ransom?

After the Battle of Poitiers in 1356, the victorious English held the French king and 2,500 knights for ransom – according to the rules of chivalry. It cost France a fortune to release them.

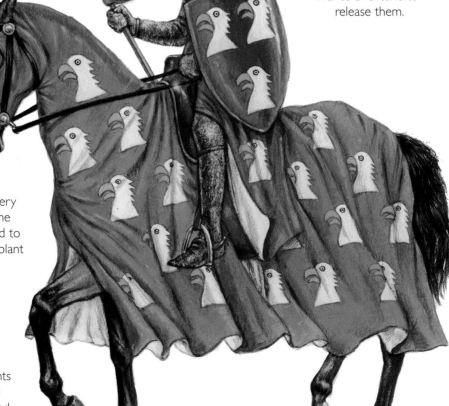

COMMAND OF THE POPES

Popes hoped to prevent tournaments by commanding that any knight killed fighting in one could not receive a Church burial. One knight got round this by changing into a monk's habit before he died from his wounds.

What was a tournament?

IT WAS A PRETEND BATTLE, IN WHICH KNIGHTS PRACTISED THEIR FIGHTING skills. The object was to capture rather than kill your opponent. You could then claim his horse and armour as a prize. Many early tournaments involved a 'mêlée', in which large teams of knights fought each other. Later, the 'joust' became more popular, in which two knights competed by riding at each other with lances.

How many people took part in a tournament?
In early tournaments as many as 3,000 mounted knights would fight in a flat meadow outside a town.

Were tournaments dangerous?
Yes, at one tournament in Cologne 60 knights died. To improve safety knights began using blunt weapons. At Windsor in 1278 the knights wore armour and helmets made from leather, and used swords made from whalebone covered in parchment and silver.

What was the tilt?
The tilt was a barrier first used in the fifteenth century to separate jousting knights. At first it was just a rope, but later a wooden barrier was used. Before the use of the tilt, collisions between jousting knights caused injuries both to knees and horses.

Richly dressed knights joust with one another. Jousting was very dangerous and many knights were fatally injured in tournaments.

Did tournaments always take place on land?

No, one contest took place on the River Thames when it froze over. At other times knights (without their horses) jousted from boats, and on one occasion horses were fitted with horse-shoes made of felt so that a tournament could take place inside a hall.

Who jousted underground?

During the siege of Montereau in 1420, mounted English and French knights jousted by torchlight in the enormous mines the English had dug beneath the French fortifications.

Noble ladies watch the jousting tournament. Many would have been watching for their special knight.

Who wore fancy dress?

MANY KNIGHTS FOUGHT AT TOURNAMENTS IN fancy dress. At Acre, in Palestine, jousting knights dressed up as nuns, women and characters from the popular story of King Arthur. At Smithfield in 1343, a team of knights dressed up as the Pope and 12 cardinals. One knight even fought wearing the dress of the lady he loved.

WILD GOOSE CHASE

In the People's Crusade, thousands of peasants marched to the Holy Land behind a preacher called Little Peter and a knight known as Walter the Penniless. Some believed hairs from the tail of Little Peter's donkey were sacred. Others followed a goose, which they said was possessed by the Holy Spirit.

What were the Crusades?

IN 1095 POPE URBAN II CALLED FOR CHRISTIAN KNIGHTS FROM

Europe to march to the Holy Land on religious 'crusades', or quests, to capture holy cities, such as Jerusalem, from the Muslims. For the next 200 years knights rode off to fight the Crusades. Knights from Europe set up their own kingdoms in the Holy Land, and built enormous castles such as Krak des Chevaliers in Syria.

Which king was never home?

Although he was king of England for ten years, Richard the Lionheart was so busy fighting and crusading that he spent only six months of this time in his own country.

What did Crusaders drink when their water ran out?

In the scorching heat of the desert, Crusaders became trapped in a castle which had no well. They were forced to drink the blood of their horses and their own urine.

Were the Crusaders cannibals?

Yes, some of these Christian warriors did eat human flesh. In 1098 starving Crusaders killed and ate their Muslim prisoners. One of them wrote: 'Our troops boiled pagan adults in cooking pots.'

Who besieged a castle full of sheep?

Richard the Lionheart

IN 1099 CRUSADERS BESIEGED A CASTLE
DEFENDED ONLY BY A FLOCK OF
sheep. The castle garrison had sneaked off during the
night, leaving their sheep behind them.

How did Crusaders give their enemies a buzz?
When the Crusaders were not having much luck firing missiles, dead
horses and severed heads from their catapults, they launched bee-hives
over the castle walls instead.

Why did old women travel with the Crusaders?
Richard the Lionheart's Crusaders travelled with groups of old women,
who cheered them on in battle, washed their bodies and clothes, and
picked the lice from their hair.

What did the Crusaders bring back from the Holy Land?
They brought back many new
things including chess, playing
cards, silk, muslin, carpets,
peacocks, windmills, rice, melons,
lemons, sugar and wheelbarrows.
In 1230 they brought back
something less pleasant – leprosy!

Crusaders built enormous castles such as this,
as they travelled through the Holy Land, trying
to convert Muslims to Christianity.

A troubadour sings and plays the cittern – an early form of guitar.

TRAIL OF THE GRAIL

Some of the greatest knightly romances concern the quest for the Holy Grail by the Knights of the Round Table. When a vision of the Grail – the cup used by Christ at the Last Supper – appears at Camelot, the knights set out to find it. Sir Galahad, the son of Lancelot, is successful in his quest because he has a pure heart.

Who recited poems about knights?

WANDERING POETS CALLED MINSTRELS OR troubadours entertained knights in their castles by reciting poems called romances. These described knights having romantic adventures in which they performed chivalrous deeds and demonstrated 'courtly love'. In this way, the stories set examples that real knights could try to follow.

Who ate her lover's heart?
In the *Châtelain de Coucy*, a famous romance, a dying knight arranges for his last letter and his heart to be sent to the woman he loves. But her husband intercepts the message, cooks the knight's heart and serves it to his wife for dinner!

Who was King Arthur?
Many romances tell the story of King Arthur. Guided by the magician Merlin, Arthur uses an enchanted sword called Excalibur to defeat his enemies. He then gathers together the most chivalrous knights in the land, who become the Knights of the Round Table.

What was courtly love?
Real knights tried to act like the knights in romances by following the ideal of 'courtly love'. They performed brave deeds in the name of a lady who they loved but could never hope to marry – usually because she was already married to somebody else!

What castle still contains a round table?
A round table from the fourteenth century still hangs in Winchester Castle. It was decorated by Henry VII, who named his own son Arthur.

Where was King Arthur's castle?
According to legend, Arthur built his queen, Guinevere, a beautiful castle called Camelot. Ruins show that the real Camelot may have been at Cadbury Castle in Somerset.

Did St George really kill a dragon?

Which real king built a round table?

The stories say that King Arthur's knights met at a round table so that no one knight had a better seat than another. When Edward III formed the Order of the Garter around 1350, he also built a round table for his knights to gather around.

Did King Arthur really exist?

The real Arthur was probably a Celtic warrior who lived in the sixth century. Many mothers named their babies Arthur at this time, probably after this man. In medieval times, story-tellers invented romantic stories about Arthur, until he became the king of legend.

Which king dug up Arthur's body?

Edward I dug up a tomb supposed to belong to Arthur and Guinevere at Glastonbury Abbey in 1278, and had the bones reburied in front of his entire court.

How did St George become patron saint of England?

The Crusaders cried out the name of St George in battle, believing the saint could protect them. When Edward III formed the Order of the Garter, St George became its patron saint. Knights wore the red cross on a white background, which was the symbol of St George, and this became the flag of England.

ACCORDING TO THE MINSTRELS' STORIES, ST GEORGE WAS A KNIGHT WHO rescued a king's daughter from a monstrous dragon. But the real St George was probably a Roman soldier who was killed around AD 303 for his Christian beliefs.

St George slays the legendary dragon.

31

Index